Bases Loaded

Great Baseball of the 20th Century

Mel Cebulash

GV
863
.A1
C423
1993

LIBRARY
NORTHERN DURHAM CENTER
Durham Technical Comm. College
2401 Snow Hill Rd.
Durham, NC 27712

New Readers Press

New Readers Press wishes to thank
The National Baseball Hall of Fame
for its help in producing this book.
Bill Deane, Research Associate

Copyright © 1993
New Readers Press
Publishing Division of Laubach Literacy International
Box 131, Syracuse, New York 13210-0131

All rights reserved. No part of this book may be
reproduced or transmitted in any form or by any
means, electronic or mechanical, including
photocopying, recording, or by any information
storage and retrieval system, without permission
in writing from the publisher.
Printed in the United States of America

Photo credit:
Pages 13 and 53 National Baseball Library
Cooperstown, N.Y.; all others AP/WIDE WORLD PHOTOS

9 8 7 6 5 4 3 2

Library of Congress Cataloging-in-Publication Data

Cebulash, Mel.
Bases loaded : great baseball of the 20th century /
Mel Cebulash.
p. cm.
ISBN 0-88336-742-4
1. Baseball—United States—History—20th century.
2. Baseball players—United States—Biography.
I. Title.
[GV863.A1C423 1993]
796.357'0973—dc20   93-432
                                             CIP

Contents

Introduction 5

The Babe of Old 7

The All-Star Returns 15

The Giant of the Giants 22

A Better Game 31

Pirates All-Star 39

Home-Run King 47

The Strikeout King Strikes 55

Introduction

By 1946, many small cities and towns had their own baseball teams. The Reds were our team in Union City, New Jersey.

Some Sundays, the Reds played in Roosevelt Stadium. Other Sundays, they played out of town.

The Reds were considered semipro. They were paid for playing, but they weren't in any league. (By the way, the general admission was 30 cents! And sometimes as many as 5,000 people came out for a game.)

I particularly remember one team that came to town—Jimmy Foxx's All-Stars.

Fresh from the big leagues, the great star was going around and playing in places like Union City just to make a few dollars. To see him in person was a great thrill for a nine-year-old. (Not many years later, Jimmy Foxx was voted into the Baseball Hall of Fame.)

In 1947, I saw my first World Series game—the Brooklyn Dodgers against the New York Yankees. The game was being shown on a TV displayed at a new store in town. I stood there and watched the game with a crowd of people. Of course, I didn't know I was also watching the end of hometown semipro baseball.

Today, the Union City Reds are long gone. So, too, are the Brooklyn Dodgers. Yet they both are part of baseball's long history. The Reds once thrilled people in a small city. The Dodgers once thrilled big-league baseball fans.

The stories in this book are also part of that long history. I hope you enjoy them, and that they stay in your memory as long as the Reds have stayed in mine.

—Mel Cebulash

Ruth calls Game-Three homer

The Babe of Old

George Herman Ruth played his first big-league game in 1914. He was 19, and he pitched for the Boston Red Sox.

The other Red Sox players quickly gave the young, baby-faced pitcher a nickname. It stuck, and George Herman Ruth soon became known around the American League as "Babe" Ruth.

The following year, Babe Ruth became a regular starting pitcher for Boston. He also showed the team something else he could do—hit home runs. In fact, he led the Sox with four home runs that season. (That's right! The hitter who led the league hit seven!)

The Babe won over 20 games for the Red Sox in 1916 and 1917. The next year, the Sox put him in the outfield for some games. As a pitcher and part-time outfielder, he hit 11 home runs—enough to lead the league.

Baseball fans were amazed by Babe Ruth's hitting. In 1919, the young pitcher, who was playing the outfield a lot now, amazed the fans even more. He hit a record 29 home runs. That year, many big-league teams didn't even hit a *total* of 29 home runs.

Before the next season started, Boston fans got some bad news. The Babe was going to be playing for the New York Yankees in 1920. The owner of the Sox had traded Babe Ruth.

With the Yankees, Babe Ruth's pitching days just about came to an end. The Yankees thought it would be better for the team if he played all the time. The Babe thought so, too. As their regular right fielder, he hit a record 54 home runs in his first year with the Yankees. It was a sign of things to come.

Year after year, Babe Ruth broke records and won games with his home-run hitting. In 1927, he raised the one-season home-run record to 60.

As more years passed, the big fellow who had started out in 1914 as a 19-year-old pitcher was not a kid anymore. Fans wondered how much longer the Babe could be the king of home runs.

Jimmy Foxx, a younger star, took over as league leader with 58 home runs in 1932. The 37-year-old Babe hit 41. He was still near the top in home runs for the season. Yet he seemed to be slowing down.

Yankee fans didn't worry about the Babe. Their team was red hot. They won 107 games that year and easily took the pennant. Over in the National League, the Chicago Cubs needed only 90 wins for their championship. The World Series was scheduled to start at Yankee Stadium. "We'll destroy the Cubs," Yankee fans said.

In Game One, the Yankees scored a 12–6 win. Yankee fans loved it. The next day, the game also went to the Yankees. This time, the score was 5–2. Both teams then took a travel break as the Series moved on to Chicago for Game Three.

The Cubs figured they could get back into the Series at home. In two games, they'd held old Babe Ruth to only two singles. Now they needed to stop the other Yankees.

Chicago fans filled Wrigley Field on October 1, 1932. They cheered when their Cubs took the field. Charlie Root started as pitcher for Chicago. During the season, the right-hander had won 15 games. Now he was going after his first World Series win.

Minutes later, Cubs fans booed the first Yankee batter as he stepped into the batter's box. "Strike him out!" they called to Root.

The Yankee hitter grounded to short. The play looked like an easy out. Then a bad throw from the shortstop got by the first baseman. When the play ended, the Yankees had a man on second base and no outs.

Being too careful, Root walked the second Yankee batter. Another Yankee headed for the batter's box. Cubs fans didn't have to hear the big, left-handed hitter's name. They knew Babe Ruth. They got on their feet and booed him. "Go home, you old bum!" some yelled.

The Babe answered the Cubs fans. He slammed one of Charlie Root's pitches deep into the stands for a home run. The Yankee fans at the game jumped up and cheered. Their team led 3–0.

The Babe batted again in the second inning. There was one Yankee on base. Trying to drive him in, Ruth slammed a fly ball deep into right field. Going back as far as he could, the Chicago outfielder pulled in the Babe's long drive.

After that, New York scored again, but the Cubs fought back. In the bottom of the fourth, they tied the score at 4–4.

Out by right field, Cubs fans fought back, too. They taunted the Babe and called him names. They were having fun, but the Babe wasn't enjoying himself. He was glad when the inning came to an end.

The first Yankee batter in the fifth inning grounded out. Again, the Cubs fans got loud as Babe Ruth walked up to the plate.

Some players on the Cubs bench got to their feet and joined in the name-calling.

The Babe pounded the plate with his big bat. Root got ready and pitched. "Strike!" the umpire called.

Looking out at the Cubs pitcher, the Babe held up a finger. "You got one strike on me," he was saying.

Watching and waiting, Ruth let the next two pitches go by. They were balls. Then Charlie Root fired a second strike past the Yankee star.

Chicago fans cheered. "Stick the next one in his ear," they called.

Root looked in for the catcher's signal. At the same time, Babe Ruth made a signal of his own. He pointed toward center field. He was going to hit the next pitch out of the ballpark.

Some Chicago fans booed. Others held their breath, hoping Babe Ruth would make a fool of himself.

The pitch came in. Ruth swung his mighty bat. The ball lifted toward center field. The Cubs outfielder started back. Then he stopped. He and 50,000 other

This painting recreates the moment when Babe Ruth pointed to center field and showed where his home run would go.

people watched the ball sail out of the park. Babe Ruth had hit his fifteenth World Series home run.

Cubs fans were shocked. They didn't want to believe their eyes. Still, they saw the old Yankee slowly going around the bases. He'd called his home run. With that swing, the old Babe had become the Babe of old once more.

Babe Ruth never hit another World Series home run. In fact, the 1932 Series was his last. The Yankees took the Series four games to none.

Three years later, Babe Ruth's playing days were over. The baby-faced young man who had started out as a Red Sox pitcher finished up as one of the greatest hitters in baseball history.

The story of Babe Ruth's marvelous feat was reported in many newspapers right after the game. No doubt, people who read the stories were as amazed as the Cubs fans who saw the home run. Even today, it seems amazing, but then so does the playing record of Babe Ruth.

Two wars can't stop Williams

The All-Star Returns

Ted Williams played right field for the Boston Red Sox in 1939. It was the first year in the big leagues for the 20-year-old from San Diego, California.

Williams batted .327 and knocked out 31 home runs that year. The Red Sox rookie also batted in 145 runs to lead both the American and National Leagues.

Two years later, Ted Williams truly amazed baseball fans. His ninth-inning home run won the 1941 All-Star game for the American League. In regular play, his 37 home runs for the season made him the big-league leader. The most amazing thing of all was his batting average for 1941.

Williams hit .406! No batter in either league came close to him.

The young man from San Diego amazed baseball fans again in 1942. This time, his .356 batting average was high enough to lead the league. He also slammed 36 home runs to top the league. To this list, he added a league-leading 137 runs-batted-in. He'd won the triple crown! He'd also become the fifth American League player ever to win all three batting titles in one year.

After the season ended, Williams made the news again. The United States was at war, and many baseball players were going into military service. Ted Williams decided he should go, too. He joined the navy.

As the war went on, the Red Sox and other teams had trouble finding good players. Most of the real All-Stars were still in the military. The 1945 All-Star game was called off. New wartime rules about travel made playing the game impossible.

Then the big news came: the war was over! Ted Williams and other baseball players got out of the service. They were excited about going back to the big leagues.

Williams had missed three years of play. Still, he was only 27. Red Sox fans figured he had many good years ahead of him. In spring training, he looked as good as ever.

With their stars back, the Boston Red Sox got off to a good start in 1946. Right away, Sox fans knew their team wasn't going to finish seventh again. Within a few weeks, the Red Sox were leading the league.

The All-Star game was scheduled for July in Boston. Red Sox fans were happy. Baseball fans around the country were happy, too. The real All-Stars were going to meet again.

A large crowd filled Fenway Park on July 9, 1946. They were proud to be on hand for the return of the All-Star game. Most of the fans in the park were from the Boston area. Their excitement about the American League's starting left fielder came as no surprise. Ted Williams was their own All-Star.

After losing for three years straight, the National League team had taken the last All-Star game in 1944. They wanted to take the 1946 game for their second win in a row. Of course, the American League stars had other ideas.

In the first inning, Williams got on base with a walk. The next American League batter hit a home run. Williams crossed the plate with the first run. At the end of one inning of play, the American League was ahead 2–0.

Williams batted again in the fourth. This time, Kirby Higbe of the Dodgers was pitching for the National League stars.

The thin Red Sox star gave Boston fans something to cheer about. He slammed one of Higbe's pitches into center field for a home run. After four innings, the American League team led 3–0.

Ted Williams singled off Higbe in inning five. By the end of the inning, the Dodger pitcher was gone, and the American League had a 6–0 lead.

In the seventh, Williams got his third straight hit—another single. The pitcher who served it up was Ewell Blackwell of the Cincinnati Reds. By the end of the inning, the American League's lead stood at 8–0.

Rip Sewell came on to pitch for the National League in the eighth. Sewell, the 39-year-old Pittsburgh pitcher, had won a lot of games during the war. He'd also come up with a strange new pitch.

Sewell called his pitch the "eephus." He tossed it up in a slow arc. As the ball moved toward the catcher, it floated down and crossed the plate.

The eephus was hard to hit. The pitch was slow, so all the power had to come from the batter. The batter also had to be patient. It wasn't easy to wait for such a slow pitch.

Rip Sewell didn't throw his eephus often. The pitch could be hit, but it couldn't be hit hard. No batter had ever homered on an eephus. Yet many had tried. Sewell waited for special times to throw his strange pitch.

Ted Williams knew about old Rip's eephus. To Williams, the pitch was a batting challenge. He wanted to get a swing at the strange pitch.

In the bottom of the eighth, Williams came up to bat for his fifth time. There were two men on base and two outs.

Rip Sewell looked in at the Red Sox star. The old pitcher knew the young hitter from San Diego wanted an eephus, so he pitched one. Williams slapped a foul ball to the left side of the field.

Sewell fired a pitch past Ted Williams for strike two. Another eephus sailed up toward the plate. It was outside, and Williams wisely let it go by.

The count was one ball and two strikes.

Sewell got ready to pitch, and Williams got ready to bat. He couldn't let another strike sneak by him. Old Rip tossed up another eephus.

Williams watched and waited. He swung. His bat slammed into the ball and lifted it toward right field. Fans got to their feet. They watched the ball go over the fence for a home run. They cheered as Ted Williams rounded the bases with his fourth straight hit.

Williams watches the ball sail out of Fenway Park.

A homer off the eephus! Two home runs in the game! Four straight hits! Four runs scored! Five runs-batted-in! Williams was back all right! So were the American League All-Stars. They won 12–0.

The 1946 All-Star game was a thrilling day in baseball. Ted Williams had many others as well. Yet no one will ever know how many he missed. In 1952, he was called back into military service for the Korean War. As a result, he missed most of the 1952 and 1953 seasons. He came back once again and played for the Red Sox until 1960. He was 42 and batted .316 that year.

Even though he had to leave to serve in two wars, Ted Williams's career was still one of the greatest in big-league history.

Mays stops one at the wall

The Giant of the Giants

In 1951, the New York Giants had a new outfielder. The 20-year-old rookie's name was Willie Mays.

Some fans liked young Willie Mays immediately. There was something about the way he played—something that showed he loved baseball.

Other fans weren't as sure about Mays. They, too, could see he loved baseball. But they wanted to see if he was up to playing in the big leagues.

By the end of the year, Willie Mays had all the fans on his side. He also had the Baseball Writers. They voted him National League Rookie of the Year. The New York rookie had batted .274 and hit 20 home runs.

Young Willie Mays got off to a bad start the following year. He batted only .236 for 34 games. He didn't make any excuses. But he certainly had something else on his mind.

Mays's second season ended after 34 games. The U.S. was at war in Korea, and Willie Mays was being called up for military service.

The 1953 season went badly for the Giants. With Mays still in the service, the team fell from second to fifth place. Fans figured the return of Willie Mays would help the team. But they guessed it would be a while before the Giants got into another pennant battle.

Willie Mays got out of the service in 1954. The Giants welcomed their young star and put him back in their starting lineup.

Fans quickly learned that military service hadn't harmed Mays. In fact, he seemed stronger and his hitting was better. The Giants were better, too—much better.

At the end of the 1954 season, the Baseball Writers gave Willie Mays another award. They named him the National League's Most Valuable Player. Mays's .345 batting average was tops in both leagues. He'd knocked out 41 home runs, too. Best of all, he'd led the Giants to a pennant win.

In the American League, the Cleveland Indians won 111 games for the pennant. The Indians had two pitchers who had won 23 games each. They had the American League batting champion and the home-run leader.

New York fans knew all about the Indians. They'd beaten a powerful Yankee team for the pennant. Beating Cleveland seemed like a big job for the Giants. But it didn't seem impossible.

Most sportswriters favored the Indians. The gamblers did too. They pointed to Cleveland's great season record. The Indians had a way of winning games—at home and on the road.

Game One of the Series was scheduled for New York's Polo Grounds. A crowd of over 50,000 filled the old ballpark. The New

York fans cheered when their team took the field.

The cheering quickly ended, as the Indians went to work. They scored two runs to take the lead in the game.

Willie Mays got up to bat in the bottom of the first. There were two Giants on base, so the fans cheered for Mays to bring them home. Mays popped out.

The Indians held their 2–0 lead until the bottom of inning three. The Giants pushed two runners across the plate to tie the score at 2–2. Mays batted in the inning, but he was walked and didn't get into the scoring.

Mays led off the bottom of the fifth and grounded out. He got up again two innings later. This time, he ended the inning by hitting into a force play. After seven full innings, the score was still tied at 2–2.

The first Indians batter in the eighth got on with a walk. He moved to second on an infield single by the next batter. Vic Wertz was next up for the Indians. In three times at bat, Vic Wertz had three hits. The hard-hitting Wertz's first-inning triple hit had knocked in Cleveland's two runs. Now he had a chance to send two more runners across home plate.

The Giants called time out. They needed another pitcher to stop Wertz. The job went to Don Liddle, a left-hander who had just finished his first year with New York.

Wertz batted left-handed. Still, the Indians had no thought of pulling him. He was hitting too well.

The New York outfielders moved in. Of course, Wertz was dangerous. He had shown he could hit the long ball. Still, the outfielders had to worry about short, pop singles. The runner on second had to be kept from scoring.

After warming up, Liddle nodded to the catcher. He was ready. Wertz, the Cleveland first baseman, stepped into the batter's box.

Liddle pitched. Wertz swung. His bat slammed into the pitch. The ball lifted out toward center field.

Willie Mays stood in place for a moment, getting his eyes on the ball. New York fans watched, too, thinking the hit looked like an easy out.

A second later, Mays turned his back on the ball and started running. He had not realized how fast the ball was moving. It almost seemed to be picking up speed and really flying. It was headed for the center-field fence. And so was the New York outfielder.

Willie Mays kept running as hard as he could. The ball was coming down, and almost like magic, he seemed to know where it would land.

Mays took a quick look over his shoulder. He set his arms in front of him. Then he raced on. He was close to the wall and knew it.

The fans held their breath. The fly ball dropped into Mays's glove. He had turned what should have been a sure hit into an out!

The cheers started immediately. But Willie Mays had no time for them. He turned and fired the ball into the infield. The runner on first raced back to his base.

The runner on second tagged up and ran to third, but got no farther. The game had been saved!

A pinch hitter's home run won the game for the Giants in the tenth. A happy crowd of New York fans left the park. They'd seen a great ending. They'd also seen one of the greatest catches in baseball history. And they also knew there wouldn't have been a tenth inning without Willie Mays's amazing catch.

The next day, sports pages showed pictures of Willie Mays stealing a hit away from Vic Wertz. He had caught it at the very deepest part of the park.

The Series went on, and the Indians played hard. Still, it seemed as if their hearts had been broken in Game One. The Giants just kept on winning. The Series ended with the Giants on top four games to none.

Four years later, the Giants and Willie Mays said goodbye to their New York fans. They moved to San Francisco.

In the 22 years he played in the big leagues, the great Willie Mays showed he

Fans look down from the bleachers as Mays makes his great game-saving catch.

could do just about whatever he wanted on a baseball field. Some years, he led the National League in home runs. Other years, he led in stolen bases. He could hit hard and run well and field what seemed like impossible hits. He proved he was the giant of the Giants.

Jackie Robinson steals home

A Better Game

Someday a woman will play big-league baseball. Some players won't like it. They'll say the game won't be the same, and they'll be right. The game will be better.

Back in 1947, some big-league players said baseball wasn't going to be the same if black men played in the majors. Many white baseball fans agreed. They said the Brooklyn Dodgers had no right to let a black man play on their team.

The man was Jackie Robinson. He was 28 years old. He'd been an All-American athlete at UCLA. He'd served in the military during World War II. He believed

31

he had a right to try. The time had come for baseball to be everybody's game.

The 1947 baseball season was hell for Jackie Robinson. He played great baseball, but many fans screamed at him anyway. They called him dirty names. They said they were going to kill him and his family. They tried many ways to hurt him. They wanted him to quit.

Many players wanted Jackie Robinson out, too. They let him know it every chance they got.

Black people watched and worried. Many probably prayed for Jackie Robinson. He'd taken on a very hard job and had to face racist attitudes every day. Yet he seemed like the man who could do it.

Robinson started at first base all through 1947. After the season, the Baseball Writers named him Rookie of the Year. He'd batted .297, and he'd led the league in stolen bases. The players and fans who had tried to stop him had failed. Slowly, some of the fans began to come around.

In time, teams in both leagues added black players. Big-league baseball got better. Now it seems impossible to imagine a team without players from all ethnic backgrounds.

In 1949, the Baseball Writers gave Jackie Robinson another award. This time, they voted him the National League's Most Valuable Player. His .342 average topped the league in batting, and his 37 stolen bases topped both leagues.

Robinson's batting average stayed well over .300 until 1955. Then his average dropped to .256, and he played in only 105 games.

Brooklyn fans knew Jackie Robinson was getting old. He had fans who had cheered him for nine years. Now he was 36, and they wondered how much playing time he had left. Some even wondered if he should be starting against the Yankees in the World Series. The Dodgers had younger stars—black and white. Fans figured these players could win the Series for the Dodgers.

Jackie Robinson wanted to play. During the season, he'd played at first base, second, third, and in the outfield. He liked to compete. Most of all, he liked to win.

Over 63,000 fans came out to Yankee Stadium for Game One of the Series. Batting seventh, Jackie Robinson started at third base for the Dodgers.

Looking like the player of his younger days, Robinson tripled in inning two. Moments later, he scored on a single.

The Yankees fought back in the bottom of the inning, scoring twice. The game was tied 2–2.

Robinson got up to bat again in the third. This time, he watched a third strike go by. Two innings later, he flied out to end the inning.

When the Dodgers got ready to bat in the eighth, the Yankees were ahead 6–3. Dodger fans cheered their first batter's single.

The next batter flied out. Then Jackie Robinson stepped up to the plate.

Robinson grounded to third. Somehow, the ball got away from the fielder. Picking up speed, Robinson stepped on first base and headed for second. The other Dodger rounded second and made his way to third. The next batter had a chance to tie the score. He hit a long fly into center field. The Yankee outfielder pulled it in for the second out. Still, the Dodger on third tagged up and scored. Robinson tagged up too and moved over to third.

The score was 6–4. Two outs. Old Jackie Robinson was on third. The Dodger pitcher was supposed to bat. But he was coming out. A pinch hitter stepped up for Brooklyn.

A hit would score Robinson. A home run would tie the game. Yogi Berra, the Yankee catcher, walked out toward the mound.

Whitey Ford was pitching for New York. He was their star pitcher. During the season, he'd led the American League with 18 wins. He also led the league with 18 complete games.

Berra handed the ball to Ford. He told Ford that he needed to be careful with the pinch hitter. He also needed to keep an eye on Robinson. The old guy could still run.

Ford knew all about Robinson's running ability. Robinson had stolen third on him in Game Six of the 1953 World Series.

After taking some practice swings, the Dodger pinch hitter stepped up to bat. Berra got ready behind the plate. He took another look at the runner on third.

Ford, the Yankee left-hander, looked over his shoulder. Robinson had taken a few steps toward home. He was watching Ford and looking as if he might try a steal.

Most fans doubted Robinson would run. Stealing home was a lot harder than stealing any other base. The Dodgers needed two runs just to tie the score. They had two outs. They wouldn't risk a third out trying to steal home.

Ford set himself. Robinson started down the line. Whitey Ford pitched. The fans got to their feet.

The pitch was outside, and the batter let it go by for a ball. Robinson stopped. He moved slowly toward the third base bag, keeping an eye on Berra.

Fans relaxed. Robinson is faking, they decided. He just wants to annoy the pitcher.

Ford got ready to pitch. Once more, Robinson took a long lead off third. Ford glanced over at Robinson. He looked back in at Berra and the batter.

A second later, Ford set himself and let his pitch go. Robinson was going too! Fans jumped to their feet. Jackie Robinson wasn't faking. He was going for home!

Near home, Robinson dropped into a slide. Berra reached for the pitch. Jackie

Jackie Robinson slides to tag the plate as he steals home base.

Robinson and the ball seemed to get there at the same time.

Robinson's foot stabbed for the plate. Berra's gloved hand hit Robinson's leg. The Yankee catcher quickly turned to the umpire. "Safe!" the umpire called, as he motioned with his hands. Jackie Robinson had stolen home!

Dodger fans cheered. Berra argued with the umpire, while some Yankee fans booed his call. Other Yankee fans clapped for Jackie Robinson. After all, he'd just made a great play.

In the end, the Yankees held their 6–5 lead and won the game. Yet the Dodgers went on to win the Series—the first for them.

After the 1956 season, Jackie Robinson retired from baseball. Later, he was voted into Baseball's Hall of Fame. This great ballplayer had made baseball a better game. He'd also made America a better country to live in.

Breaking the five-year rule

Pirates All-Star

Roberto Clemente grew up in Puerto Rico. He started playing baseball at an early age. He loved the game, and by the time he reached high school, he was a good player.

Soon big-league scouts heard about Roberto Clemente. They came to Puerto Rico to see if he was as good as people said he was. A few scouts saw all they needed to see. They told their teams to try to get Clemente.

After graduation, Clemente signed on with Montreal. At the time, Montreal was a Dodger farm team.

Clemente quickly got the attention of other big-league teams. They had scouts check out Montreal's new player.

In November of 1954, the Pittsburgh Pirates drafted the young man from Puerto Rico. They thought the 20-year-old was just about ready for big-league play.

Clemente joined the Pirates in 1955 and almost immediately became their starting right fielder. He broke no rookie records that year. Still, he hit .255 and showed signs that he would improve as he got older.

In fact, he improved his hitting quite a bit in his second year of big-league play. His .311 batting average made him third in the league.

Clemente's average fell below .300 for the next three seasons. Still, his hitting satisfied the Pirates. They kept him in his starting spot in right field.

In 1960, Clemente jumped way up in his climb to be a big star. He was 25 and a much better player. He was picked for his first All-Star team. For the season, he hit .314 and batted in 94 runs.

The Pirates had a good year, too. They went from fourth place to first in the National League. Then they beat the

Yankees 4–3 for the world title. Clemente batted .310 for the Series.

The Pirates didn't play like World Champions in 1961. Roberto Clemente played like a champion anyway. Again, he got picked for a starting place on the All-Star team. Back in Puerto Rico, his family and friends were thrilled. So were his fans in Pittsburgh.

On July 11, more than 44,000 fans crowded into San Francisco's Candlestick Park for the All-Star Game. It was hot that afternoon.

The heat didn't bother Clemente. He came up in the second inning with nobody on base. Facing Yankee ace Whitey Ford, he slammed a hard line drive into the outfield.

Roger Maris, another Yankee All-Star, chased after Roberto Clemente's long hit. When the play ended, Clemente was on third with a triple.

Moments later, a sacrifice fly sent Roberto Clemente home. His run gave the National League a 1–0 lead.

Clemente batted again in the fourth inning. This time, Willie Mays was on third.

There was one out. Dick Donovan, a right-hander from the Washington Senators, was pitching.

Clemente went after an outside pitch and punched a fly into right field. The American League fielder made the catch. Mays tagged on the sacrifice fly and scored. Clemente had batted in the run, and the National League had a 2–0 lead.

The American League team wasn't ready to quit. Behind 3–1 after eight innings, they fought back with some help from the weather at Candlestick Park.

By the ninth inning, the hot weather had changed to windy and warm. The strong wind meant trouble for the National League fielders. They made some costly errors.

Taking advantage of the poor fielding, the American League scored twice in the inning.

The National League failed to score in the bottom of the ninth. The game was tied 3–3.

Poor fielding helped the American League team again in the tenth. They scored a run on a bad throw. They moved into the bottom of the tenth with a 4–3 lead.

Hoyt Wilhelm was pitching for the American League. Hoyt, a knuckleball ace, was a great relief pitcher.

Hank Aaron led off the tenth inning with a single. He moved to second base when one of Hoyt's knuckleballs got away from the catcher.

Seconds later, Willie Mays doubled. Aaron raced all the way home and tied the score at 4–4.

A Hoyt pitch hit the next batter, sending him to first. National League fans cheered. Roberto Clemente was up next.

With no outs and two on, fans guessed Clemente would be bunting. They quickly learned otherwise. Clemente took a hard cut, missing Hoyt's first pitch.

Hoyt tossed up his knuckleball. It was outside. Clemente reached out and slapped the pitch into right field.

Running on the hit, Mays rounded third and rolled home. The game was over! Roberto Clemente had knocked in the winning run for the National League.

Along with being an All-Star hero in 1961, Clemente won the batting title with a .351 average. He'd become a great player, and he was still young enough to be one of the greatest ever.

Clemente won the batting title again in 1964 and 1965. The following year, the Baseball Writers gave him another title—Most Valuable Player in the National League.

In 1967, Clemente took another batting title with a .357 average. He was 33 years old, but he wasn't slowing down.

Pittsburgh fans had more to cheer about in 1971. This time, Clemente led the Pirates to a World Series win over Baltimore. He batted .414 and hit two home runs in the seven games. Once again, he won an award—Most Valuable Player of the World Series.

Clemente celebrated his thirty-eighth birthday in 1972. It was his eighteenth year with the Pirates. He batted .312 and made his last hit of the year his 3,000th.

On New Year's Eve of 1972, baseball fans got some bad news. People in Puerto Rico

Roberto Clemente, the Pirates All-Star, was both a Series and a League MVP.

had given food to help poor people in Nicaragua. Roberto Clemente had hired a plane to take the food to Nicaragua. He helped load it. Then he took off on the flight, expecting to help unload after landing.

The plane never landed. It had crashed into the sea. The great Roberto Clemente was missing.

By the next day, a huge search was started. People prayed, but no one held much hope for Clemente and the others who had been on the plane.

Finally, the word came. Roberto Clemente was dead. He'd lost his life on his way to help others. His last hit of the season, his 3,000th hit, had been the last hit of his life. It was tragic news, especially for people in Pittsburgh and Puerto Rico.

Early in 1973, Roberto Clemente was named to baseball's Hall of Fame. By the rules, a player couldn't be voted in until five years after he stopped playing. In this case, Roberto Clemente was just about a sure thing to make the Hall. So the Writers decided to break the five-year rule. Clemente's fans were happy with the decision, though they still mourned the loss of Clemente.

Hank Aaron breaks The Record

Home-Run King

Hank Aaron grew up in Alabama. In 1954, he played in his first big-league game. He was only 20 years old. The year before, he had played second base in the minor leagues. Now he was the starting left fielder for the Milwaukee Braves of the National League.

Throughout his rookie year, young Hank Aaron showed he could hit big-league pitching. By the end of the season, he'd batted .280 and hit 13 home runs.

In each of the next five years, Hank Aaron's batting average was well over the .300 mark. In two of those years, he led the National League in batting. Along the way, he became a star.

Aaron's home-run hitting went up along with his batting average. In 1957, he led both leagues with 44 homers. That year, the Baseball Writers named him the National League's Most Valuable Player.

Six years later, Hank Aaron again ended a season with 44 home runs. This time, he had to settle for a tie with another hitter for the National League lead.

The Braves moved to Atlanta in 1966. Aaron's batting average dropped below .300 that season. It was the first time in years he'd been under the .300 mark. His long-time fans weren't worried, though. He still belted out 44 home runs—enough once again to lead the National League.

Number 44 of the Braves, Hank Aaron again blasted 44 baseballs out of the park in 1969. For the season, he was only one home run behind the league leader.

Fans began to take a long look at Aaron's lifetime record. After 16 seasons, he had knocked out more than 500 home runs in big-league play. Hank Aaron was going to be one of the best home-run hitters in baseball history.

Some fans were even starting to think of Hank Aaron becoming the new home-run king of baseball. The record of 714 belonged to Babe Ruth. Aaron was only 35 years old. Maybe, just maybe, he had enough years left to catch up to the Babe.

In 1971, Aaron played first base in more games than he played in the outfield. The change in position didn't bother his hitting. He hit 47 home runs, missing the league lead by one. Still, the 47 homers were the most he'd ever hit in one season.

Now Hank Aaron had 639 home runs.

He was in third place on the list of all-time home-run hitters. Another player in the league had 646 homers. Like Aaron, the player in second place had also grown up in Alabama. His name was Willie Mays.

With 34 four-baggers, Hank Aaron moved into second place in 1972. At 41, Mays was about through with big-league ball. Now Hank Aaron only had to top Babe Ruth to become the all-time home-run king.

The 1972 season marked the twenty-sixth year since Jackie Robinson had entered the big leagues. In 1947, he had opened the door. Now the big leagues were filled with great African-American players.

Baseball had changed, but some people hadn't changed with it. Hank Aaron in time found that out.

Aaron started the 1973 season needing only 42 home runs to top Babe Ruth's record. To his many fans, black and white, he was the greatest home-run hitter who ever lived. They just sat back and waited for the day he would become the all-time leader.

Other people were also watching Hank Aaron. They were sick people filled with hate. They wrote terrible letters to Aaron. They called him names. They threatened him. They even threatened his family.

Some of these people called on the phone. They told Hank Aaron he should quit baseball—for his own good.

Hank Aaron didn't let these people get to him. He answered them by playing another good season. In July, he hit his 700th home run. Now only foolish people doubted Aaron would pass Babe Ruth.

But these people kept after Hank Aaron. They continued sending hate-filled letters, and they cursed him at the ballparks.

By the end of the season, Hank Aaron had knocked out 40 home runs. He'd raised his total to 713. He was only one short of a tie with Babe Ruth!

The people who were harassing Aaron created problems. They'd caused the Braves to hire people to protect their great star. They'd caused Aaron to worry about his family. Yet they didn't scare Hank Aaron. Nor did they stop him.

Photographers and writers began to follow Hank Aaron everywhere now. He was about to become the greatest home-run hitter in baseball history. He was big news.

The Braves played their first game of 1974 in Cincinnati. A huge crowd came out for opening day. They were fans of the Reds. Yet many of them hoped to see Aaron break the home-run record. Instead, they only saw him tie it—with a first-inning blast.

Hank Aaron sat out game two. Back in Atlanta, his fans hoped he would sit out game three, too. Then he could return to his home field for the record-breaker.

Aaron played seven innings in game three. He batted three times, but failed to hit one out of the park. Atlanta fans were probably happy. It meant Hank Aaron was coming home.

On April 8, 1974, the minds of baseball fans all over America fixed on Atlanta. Over 53,000 people filled the stadium. All the big TV networks sent reporters and cameras to cover the story.

Hank Aaron's next home run was going to be the biggest event in baseball since Jackie Robinson's first big-league game.

The Dodgers picked left-hander Al Downing to pitch against the Braves. Excited fans roared at every throw. But Downing walked Aaron to start inning two.

Hank Aaron came up again in the fourth. This time he slammed Downing's second pitch into left field for a home run. The fans jumped to their feet and cheered. Hank Aaron slowly went around the bases

Aaron watches as Home Run Number 715 goes out of the ballpark and into history.

for his 715th home run. He was the new home-run king!

Across the country, millions of people cheered. For years, people had said no one could break Babe Ruth's record. Aaron had done it! Even with people harassing him, Aaron had done it! Of course, the game stopped for a while. He was given a watch in honor of his record-breaker.

Hank Aaron hit 18 more home runs that year. By the time he decided to call it quits in 1976, he had 755 home runs. His record may never be broken. In fact, Aaron has two other hitting records that may never be broken. He batted in 2,297 runs in his playing days. He also made 1,477 extra-base hits. He was truly the king of the long ball.

Reggie Jackson's home-run streak

The Strikeout King Strikes

Reggie Jackson became a baseball star with the Oakland Athletics. He played right field and made fans happy with his powerful home runs.

In 1973, the Baseball Writers named Jackson the American League's Most Valuable Player. Over the year, he led the league with 117 runs-batted-in and 32 home runs. He also led his team to a league title.

The Writers also gave Jackson the 1973 World Series Most Valuable Player award. His hitting helped the Athletics win the Series.

Jackson was traded to Baltimore in 1976. He played one season there—his tenth in

The Reggie Jackson home-run swing, in a 1977 World Series game.

the big leagues. After that, Jackson signed up with the New York Yankees.

Most baseball fans in New York were excited by the news. Reggie Jackson already had 281 home runs. He was only 30 years old. Fans figured he'd hit lots of homers for the Yankees.

But some fans worried about Jackson's strikeouts. He usually struck out over 100 times a season. He was on his way to becoming the strikeout king of the big leagues.

Reggie Jackson wasn't worried, though. He enjoyed taking big, hard swings. He also figured the Yankees were paying him to hit home runs—not cut down on his strikeouts.

New York fans learned a lot about Reggie Jackson in 1977. He did like to swing. He hit 32 home runs and struck out 129 times. Yet even in striking out, Jackson had the style of a champion. Reggie Jackson's left-handed swing was beautiful to watch. It was exciting. It had "home run" written all over it—even when he missed.

After the season, the Yankees beat Kansas City for the American League Title.

As for Jackson, he batted only .125 for the series and failed to get an extra-base hit.

Yankee fans figured Jackson would hit better against the Los Angeles Dodgers. They cheered when he went to right field for the start of the 1977 World Series.

Over 56,000 fans filled Yankee Stadium that opening day. They saw an exciting game which was tied after nine innings. A run in the twelfth gave the Yankees a 4–3 win.

Jackson got one hit—a pop single in the first inning. The next day, he failed to get a hit and struck out twice. Meanwhile, the Dodgers tied the Series with a 6–1 win.

Two days later, a huge crowd in Los Angeles watched the Dodgers lose 5–3. This time, Jackson batted in a run with a single. He also struck out twice.

Another huge Los Angeles crowd came out for Game Four. As usual, Jackson was swinging. Only this time, he wasn't missing.

Jackson hit a double his first time at bat. In the sixth inning, he slammed a long home run. He flied out his other two times at bat. In the end, the Yankees won 4–2.

They were one game away from being World Champions.

The Dodgers fought back in Game Five and walked off with a 10–4 win. Again, Jackson got two hits and didn't strike out. His second hit of the game was also his second homer of the Series.

The teams traveled back to New York. Once more, the Dodgers had to win—or the Series was over. They picked Burt Hooton as their starting pitcher. He'd beaten the Yankees in the second game of the Series.

Fans crowded into Yankee Stadium for Game Six. The Dodgers quickly showed them why they were National League Champions. They scored two runs in the first inning.

Jackson came to bat in inning two. His fans cheered as Hooton walked him on four pitches. The next New York batter homered and the score was tied 2–2.

The Dodgers answered with a home run in inning three and took a 3–2 lead. In the bottom of the inning, Hooton sent the next three Yankees back to the dugout.

Jackson batted again in the fourth. This time, there were no outs and a runner on first. Jackson's fans shouted to him. They wanted him to hit one out.

Burt Hooton got set and pitched. Jackson wasted no time swinging away. Fans jumped to their feet. They watched the drive take off. It sailed into the right-field seats. A home run! Fans cheered as Jackson rounded the bases.

The Dodgers quickly pulled Hooton, but the damage had been done. The Yankees now had the lead.

Jackson got another turn at bat in the fifth inning. This time, the Yankees had two outs and a runner on first base.

Leading 5–3, the New York team wanted more runs to be safe. The New York fans just wanted more runs. They screamed for Jackson to do it again.

Elias Sosa was pitching for the Dodgers. Jackson dug in, taking a long, hard look at the Los Angeles right-hander. Sosa fired a fastball, and Jackson blasted it into right field. Another home run! Jackson's fourth of the Series!

As Jackson rounded the bases, some fans eyed the scoreboard. The Yankees were now going to be leading 7–3. The Dodgers were in big trouble.

Other fans just cheered and kept their eyes on Reggie Jackson. He'd taken two

Jackson about to make contact with his record-breaking third home run.

swings in the game and hit two homers. His first-inning walk didn't count as a turn at bat. So he had hit three homers in his last three ups in the Series.

The Dodgers failed to score over the next three innings. They had three outs left, but they had to stop the Yankees in the eighth.

As soon as the inning started, Yankee fans stood up and cheered for Reggie Jackson. They seemed to be showing him how proud they were of him.

Charlie Hough was pitching for Los Angeles. Hough, a knuckleball pitcher, had struck out two Yankees in the seventh inning.

He'd also struck out Jackson the only time he'd faced him in Game Three.

As always, Jackson took some giant practice swings. Then he stepped in and set himself.

Hough got ready and pitched. The knuckleball came up, and Jackson went after it. His bat tore into the ball. It roared off, as Yankee fans roared with excitement.

Jackson, the catcher, and the umpire watch the ball fly out of the park to become Jackson's fourth homer in a row.

Finally, the ball dropped down into the center-field seats. Another home run!

Reggie Jackson slowly ran the bases. He wore a big smile. He was enjoying the moment. He had struck—his third homer in the game and fourth homer in a row.

The Dodgers scored a run in the ninth. Of course, it wasn't enough. The Yankees were the World Champions once again.

Reggie Jackson won the World Series Most Valuable Player award. It was the second time he'd won the award.

Reggie Jackson was elected to the Baseball Hall of Fame in 1993. In all, he played for 21 seasons. He hit 563 home runs. He also struck out 2,597 times. His strikeout record may never be broken. But no one who saw him play will ever forget his beautiful swing.